Astronauts
Take Flight

By Robert Gott

Contents

Sailors of the Stars

Astronaut means "sailor of the stars". Like sailors long ago, astronauts want to find out what is out there.

Astronauts are brave. They know that space travel is dangerous. Yet, they believe it is worth the risk. In this book, you will read about five brave astronauts.

This astronaut crew is about to begin a space shuttle mission.

Andrew S W Thomas

born 1951

> "If I could
> go to the Moon,
> I would do so
> in an instant!"

When Andy Thomas was a child he saw the first satellite launched from Earth into space. It was called *Sputnik 1*. As Andy looked into the sky, he saw *Sputnik 1* pass overhead. From that moment he became interested in space and rockets.

When Andy grew up, he became a scientist. He studied space and flight for many years. By 1990 he was well known for his work.

In 1992 the National Aeronautics and Space Administration (NASA) chose Andy to be an astronaut. After his training, Andy was ready for space travel.

In 1996 Andy went on his first spaceflight. He was the first Australian to travel in space.

After that, Andy trained in Russia for a visit to a space station called *Mir*. He also learned Russian so he could talk to the crew.

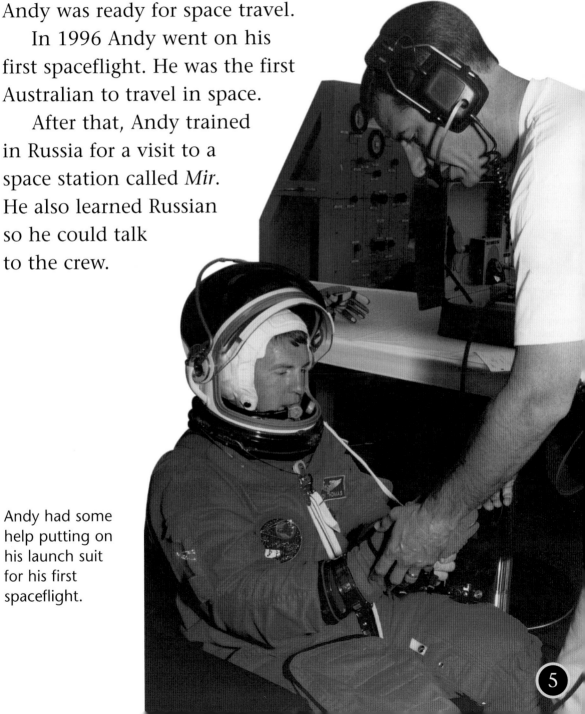

Andy had some help putting on his launch suit for his first spaceflight.

On *Mir*, Andy ran on a treadmill to keep fit.

Andy and the crew lived on *Mir* for four months. Each astronaut had a job to do. Andy's job was to find out how space travel affects the human body.

Mir was quite small, but Andy liked it. There was a living area, an exercise area and small sleeping areas for the astronauts. Andy slept in a sleeping bag that was tied in place to stop him from floating around.

⭐ Eating in Space

Imagine eating in a place where everything floats. Let go of a cereal spoon and it floats away. This would be a problem if tiny food crumbs floated off. They could get stuck in an astronaut's eyes or interfere with equipment. To help astronauts, food is carefully prepared.

In 2001 Andy travelled to the International Space Station (ISS). There, he became the first Australian to walk in space. He helped to prepare the ISS for a new crew. He added parts to the outside of the ISS with another crew member. Together they made a platform to hold a robotic arm from Canada. Andy received many awards when he returned from space.

International Space Station

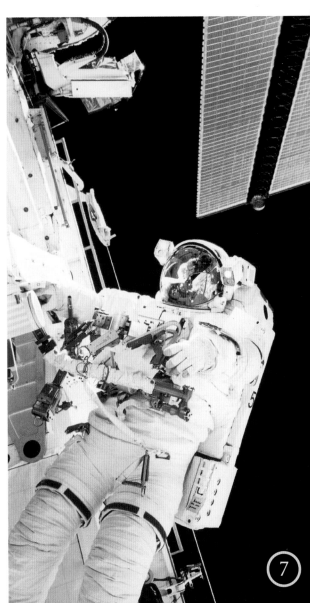

This is Andy on a spacewalk during his mission to the International Space Station.

Michael P Anderson

born 1959, died 2003

"I take the risk because I think what we are doing is really important."

Michael Anderson grew up near airfields where aeroplanes took off and landed all the time. This made him very interested in flying. Michael was nine years old when the first astronaut walked on the Moon. He watched the moonwalk on television. He decided that one day he too would be an astronaut.

In 1981 Michael became a pilot in the US airforce. Then he taught other pilots how to fly, too.

In 1994 NASA chose Michael to be an astronaut. He trained hard, and by the next year was ready for space travel.

In 1998 Michael went on his first spaceflight on the space shuttle *Endeavour*.

Michael with other crew members.

Michael was on an important mission. He and the crew had to take Andy Thomas to space station *Mir*. They also had to deliver supplies to the space station.

In 2003 Michael was chosen for a mission on the space shuttle *Columbia*. It was a science mission. Michael was in charge of the science experiments.

★★

⭐ Supplies to *Mir*

Michael Anderson was on space shuttle *Endeavour* for its first docking mission with *Mir*. *Endeavour*'s crew delivered more than 4,000 kilograms of supplies and equipment to *Mir*.

Michael set up an experiment on space shuttle *Columbia* in 2003.

Tragically the mission did not end as planned. On 1st February 2003 the space shuttle broke apart while returning to Earth. All seven members of the *Columbia* crew died.

Michael Anderson is remembered as a hero. He worked hard and did not give up when faced with great challenges.

Helen Sharman

born 1963

"Science opens up new opportunities every day."

Helen Sharman never thought that she would become the first astronaut from the UK to go into space. Helen loved science. She studied chemistry at Sheffield University.

Her first job was making equipment for ships, aircraft and hospitals. Helen loved her job because she could use her science skills.

One day, Helen heard an advertisement on the radio: "Astronaut wanted, no experience needed." Russia and the UK were gathering a crew for a space mission called Project Juno. They were looking for someone to be the first person from the UK in space. They wanted a calm person who worked well with others. They also had to be strong and healthy. Helen had all of these qualities.

★ Helen's Passport and Clothes

Helen took a space passport on her mission. She would have needed it if she had landed in certain countries on return to Earth.

Helen's flight suit

Helen's space passport

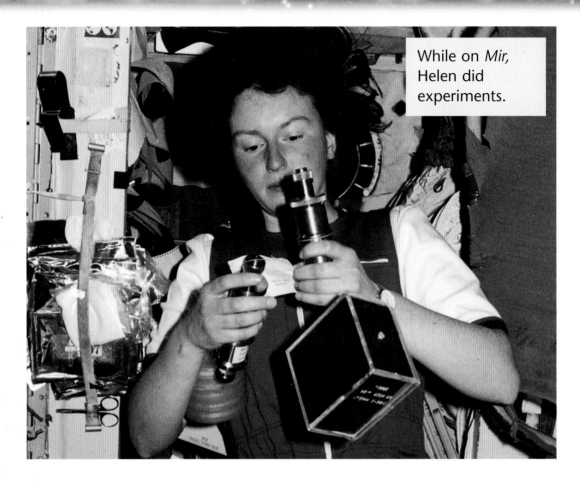

While on *Mir*, Helen did experiments.

Helen was chosen from among 13,000 people to be the first astronaut from the UK. In 1989 she was sent to Russia for training. There, she learned to speak Russian. She also learned how to do experiments in space. In 1991 she and two Russian astronauts, called cosmonauts, were launched into space.

Helen spent six days on *Mir*. While in space, Helen studied how weightlessness affects people and plants.

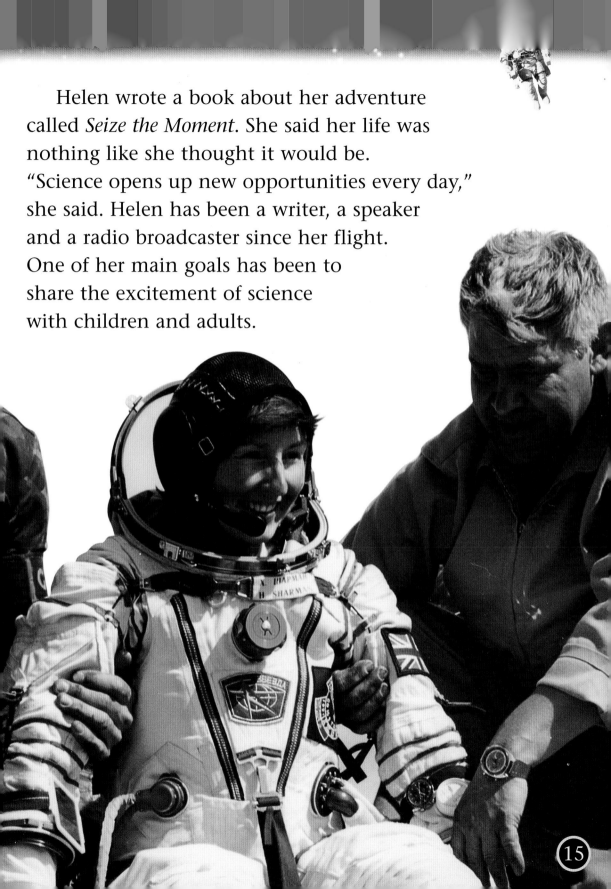

Helen wrote a book about her adventure called *Seize the Moment*. She said her life was nothing like she thought it would be. "Science opens up new opportunities every day," she said. Helen has been a writer, a speaker and a radio broadcaster since her flight. One of her main goals has been to share the excitement of science with children and adults.

Marc Garneau

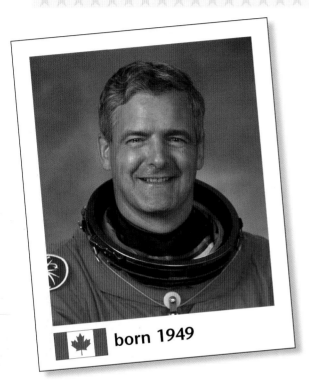

born 1949

"Going into space alters your perception... You realize how important it is to take care of our planet."

In 1983 Marc Garneau had a good job in the Canadian Navy. He was very happy and didn't think he would change his job. Then the United States invited Canada to send an astronaut on the space shuttle *Challenger*. Marc was one of the six people chosen for training in the new Canadian programme.

Marc on one of his space shuttle missions.

Marc spent eight days in space on his flight in 1984. He did experiments in medicine. He also studied how robots work in space. Marc worked hard to help make the Canadian astronaut programme a success when he returned to Earth.

★★★★★★★★★★★★★★★★★

⭐ Space Robots

Robots are used to explore space and to fix space stations. They do dangerous tasks so astronauts don't have to. They can also do jobs that take many hours without becoming tired. Sprint is a robotic camera that takes photos in space without becoming tired.

Sprint

Marc loved his space adventure and wanted to fly in space again. In 1992 he was chosen by NASA to enter a special training programme. He learned how to use many of the systems on a space shuttle.

In 1996 Marc made his second flight. He spent ten days on the space shuttle *Endeavour*. His third flight was also on the *Endeavour*. This time he helped build the International Space Station (ISS).

A parachute helped to slow down *Endeavour* on its return to Earth.

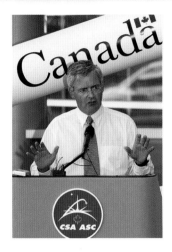

In 2001 Marc became president of the Canadian Space Agency (CSA). Now he helps decide which projects the CSA will do and how they will do them. One of Marc's goals is for Canada to become an important part of future missions to Mars.

In 2003 Marc spoke about Canada's plans for more space exploration.

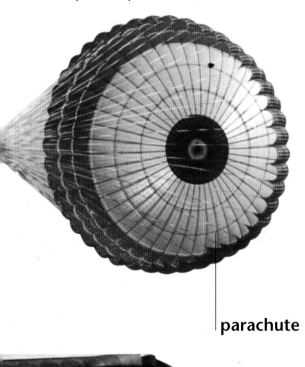

parachute

France   India

Romania   Mongolia

19

Ellen Ochoa

born 1958

"Only you put limitations on yourself about what you can achieve. Don't be afraid to reach for the stars!"

Dr Ellen Ochoa became the first Mexican American woman to fly in space. Ellen always loved maths. She was an excellent student at her university. There she helped invent equipment that scientists use to look at images from space.

In 1990 NASA chose Ellen to be an astronaut. Her maths and science skills helped her as she studied and trained hard.

In 1993 Ellen went on her first spaceflight to the International Space Station (ISS).

Ellen played the flute for the crew on space shuttle *Discovery*.

⭐ **Space Equipment**

Astronauts have to learn how to use all kinds of equipment inside and outside the spacecraft. Ellen worked the controls for the robotic arm Canadarm on several space missions.

On Ellen's first mission she captured a
satellite that had been studying the Sun.
She used Canadarm to capture it.

In 1999 Ellen and other astronauts went
to the ISS. They prepared it for the first crew
to live there. In 2002 Ellen made another
trip to the ISS.

Today Ellen works at the Johnson Space Centre in Houston, Texas. She communicates with space shuttles and helps to guide astronauts in space. Her goal is to improve the ISS. Ellen also enjoys talking to students about her adventures.

Ellen and another astronaut floated in one of the experiment rooms in the International Space Station.

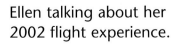
Ellen talking about her 2002 flight experience.

Index